JUMBLED

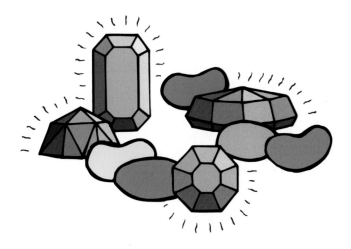

Written by Betty Neal
Illustrated by Margaret Willis and Jeff McKellar

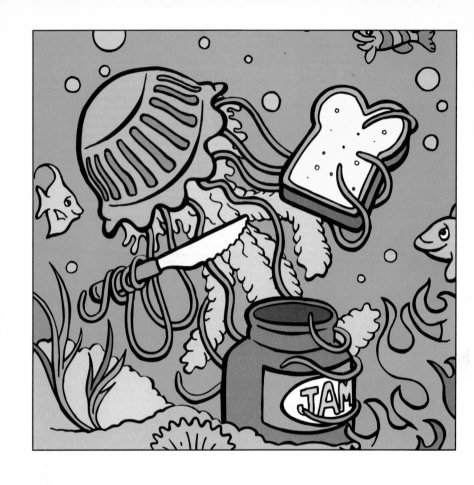

Jellyfish jam.

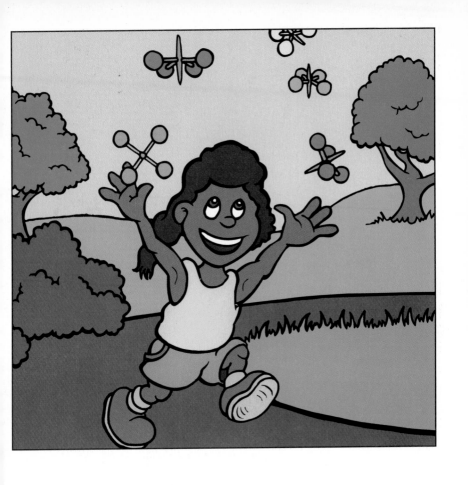

Jogger juggling jacks.

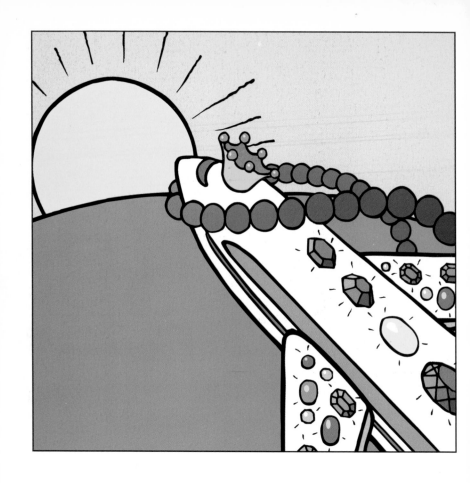

Jewels on a jet.

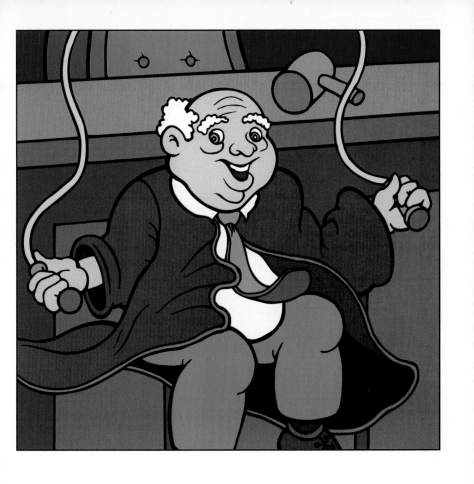

Judge jumping rope.

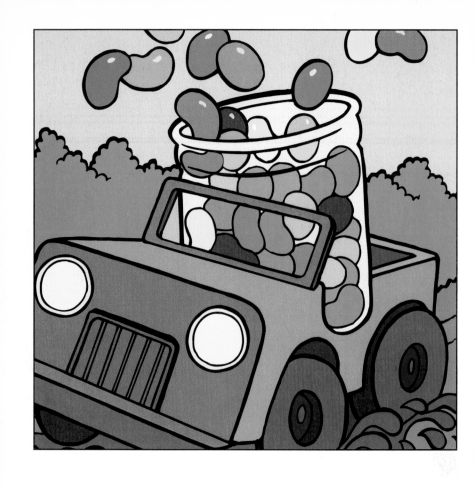

Jeep with jelly beans.

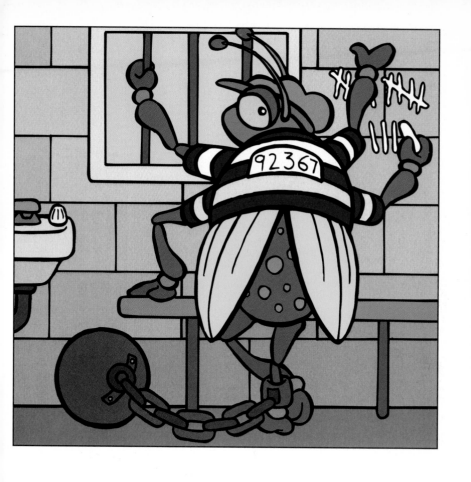

June bug in jail.

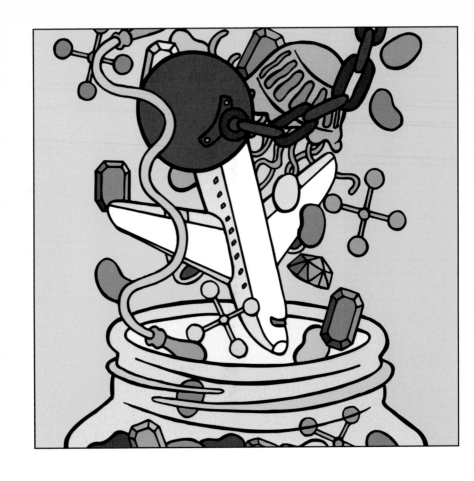

Everything is jumbled!